MW01659549

When Faith Becomes Glory

Cheryl L. Black

Christian Living™ BOOKS

Christian Living Books, Inc.
An imprint of Pneuma Life Publishing
Largo, MD

ISBN 1-56229-008-8

Printed in the United States of America

Unless otherwise marked all Scripture quotations are taken from the King James Version of the Bible.

Excerpts taken from the following messages: *The Power of Knowing When Faith Becomes Glory*, *The Spirit of Glory is Resting upon You*, and *It's the Right Time.* Used with permission of Bishop Noel Jones.

Christian Living Books, Inc.
An imprint of Pneuma Life Publishing, Inc.
P. O. Box 7584
Largo, MD 20792
301-218-9092
www.christianlivingbooks.com

Dedication

This book is dedicated to my five children whom I love dearly. God blessed me with every one of you. He used you to help make and mold me into the woman He wanted me to be.

You all are so uniquely different which caused a real challenge for me. You brought out the worst in me and the best in me. Either way, it caused me to grow. You helped me to mature. You caused me to look at myself and say, "I don't want to be like that; or it's ok to be myself in other ways." And, I thank the Lord for helping me to change. He not only changed me, but He gave me strength I didn't know I could have.

It is because of you that I learned how to pray. It is because of you that I fought to hold onto my mind. It is because of you that I have a story to tell. He entrusted me with you to train up according to His Word; and I did the best that I knew how.

As you know, my prayer for you is that you will be saved. I want you to always remember what He said:

> *If we* ***confess*** *our sins, he is faithful and just to forgive us our sins, and to cleanse us from all unrighteousness.* (I John 1:9)

Christ died for you the same as He died for me. Always remember that God loves you, no matter what. He just wants you to love Him back. If you trust Him, He won't fail you because He is faithful that promised!

Love,
Mama

Father,

Be glorified in this book you have placed within me to write. I give You all the glory, the honor and all the praise, in Jesus name. Amen!

Table of Contents

Preface

This book is not about me. I just happen to be the person chosen to have these experiences so that I could share them with you. It is all about God and His faithfulness to His Word. It is about the truth of His Word. It is about God being glorified in the lives of ordinary people who put their complete trust in Him.

It is my desire to show you clusters of faith, shining brightly at some points in my life. It is about the awesomeness of God, Who is *our very present help in time of trouble.*

As you read, I pray God give you renewed strength and courage to go through the multitude of struggles and perplexing situations that life brings your way. I pray He will fortify you, so when the storms come, you will be able to stand. I pray you will remember every word and every promise that He has given to us. I pray that God will not only increase your faith, but that He will give you unwavering faith. I pray He will give you faith to make it through the storms.

Acknowledgments

I want to acknowledge and thank all of my family–every aunt, uncle and cousin–for your love and support. I appreciate you all so very much. I want to acknowledge my grandparents, Mother Adell Anderson and the late Elder Arthur J. Anderson. They raised me, brought me up in the church, and taught me the fear of the Lord.

I especially want to give thanks to my mother, Thelma Morris, who worked so hard to provide for me and my two sisters. Mama, I love and appreciate you. I want my sisters, Paulette and Linda, to know I love you both very much. To my dad and other mom, Hubert Johnson and Josie, thank you for being there when I needed you.

I want to thank Pastor C. T. Anderson and Sister Barbara for all of your teaching and nurturing and, for every sacrifice you made on my behalf. I want to thank every member of Greater Rose of Sharon for your love and support through the years.

To my best friend, Beryl Stewart, who has been a friend through all of our struggles of raising our children: I love you. Thank you for being there for me. To Clint and Harold McRae of Two Brothers Auto Shop, thank you for keeping every car that I had running for as long as I needed. And, thank you for coming to get me whenever and wherever I got stranded–in the rain or snow.

Thanks to my very special friends, Morris Fierberg and Larry Woods. Without your counsel and friendships I would not have learned some very important lessons. Morris, I want to thank you for your patience with me, also for your listening ear and tender heart. Larry, I thank you for being man enough to talk to my sons about men issues. And I thank you for attending every function that was important to Jennifer as a young woman. You have been a wonderful godfather. I'm grateful to God for allowing me to know men of integrity and strength.

I want to give special thanks to Jimmy and Yvette Moore, who believed God enough to take me into their home when I accepted God's challenge to move to California.

To my former roommate, Florence Duvall, thank you for your kindness to a stranger; and, my late in life dormitory experience.

To Cory Briggs, thank you for your friendship and respect and for sharing your family with me– especially your mom. Father God, I thank you for the life of Annisue Briggs. I thank you for allowing us to share for a little while. I'll never forget her kindness and words of encouragement to me. Desiree and J, I love you both.

To my pastor, Bishop Noel Jones, thank you for the words of wisdom and encouragement you give to me through the preached Word of God. I thank God for your life and the ministry that He has placed within you. I thank God for directing me to City of Refuge, formerly known as Greater Bethany Community Church, when I needed a church home and a sense of belonging. My thanks to every member who has shown his or her kindness to me.

And to everyone I didn't mention by name–friend or foe–my love and appreciation goes to you too!

Tried Faith

1

It was January 1989 when I received the most terrifying telephone call of my life. I was at work; and, my manager came over to me and said she needed to see me in the conference room. I wondered what I did. She said, "Cheryl, your son's Commanding Officer [CO] of the Marine Corp is on the phone." My heart sank. She asked me if I wanted her to stay. I said yes.

He said to me, Miss Black your son is in jail. He killed someone. I broke down crying. I said, "No, not my son. He wouldn't do anything like that." His CO said, I'm sorry to say but he did. He called me and told me himself and asked me to come and pick him up. His CO sent some military police to the scene. I asked him where my son was. He was being held at the Jacksonville, North Carolina police station. "Whenever you make arrangements to come to Jacksonville, call me," he said. "I'll have someone meet you at the airport. We'll make arrangements for you to have somewhere to stay." I was devastated!

My supervisor said she would have someone drive me home because she was afraid for me to drive in that condition. I told her I would make it. She insisted on calling my family. I had her to call my pastor, who is also my uncle, and to have him to meet me at my house. He said he would be there. Someone drove me home. My pastor was there and I informed him of everything I had been told. I prepared to go to Jacksonville, North Carolina–a place I had never been before. I was praying everyday.

I went to church the Sunday before I left Detroit. I remember singing, "The Lord is my Light and my Salvation." I sung until the Lord came in and lifted me. The song says, "In the time of trouble, He shall hide me." At that point, I think some of my family thought I was going to have a nervous breakdown. They know how close I am to my sons. But, I wasn't going to have a nervous breakdown. It wasn't the time, and I didn't have that on my mind. My child was in serious trouble and he needed his mama. I needed to go and see about him; and, the Lord was going to make a way. The Lord was going to have to take us through, because my family had never dealt with this kind of situation before.

ANXIOUS AND CONCERNED

My first trip to North Carolina was very difficult because I had never been to the South. My son was the only person I knew in Jacksonville and he was in jail. A young woman had called me and said my son told her to call me. She said she was his friend and I could stay with her. She wanted to know when I would be coming; so, I told her. She offered to pick me up at the airport, but I told her the CO had made arrangements to have a military policeman from my son's unit pick me up. I said I would call her whenever I got there.

I had heard some bad things concerning Jacksonville and I felt really scared and anxious at times, but I was going. I heard about the prejudice–and about the skinheads being a real threat to people there. The enemy was really trying to sow seeds of fear in my mind. But the Word of God kept coming up in my spirit.

> *For the word of God is quick and powerful and sharper than any two-edged sword, piercing even to the dividing asunder of soul and spirit, and of the joints and marrow, and is a discerner of the thoughts and intents of the heart.* (Hebrews 4:12)

The Holy Ghost was definitely working to bring every word I had ever heard back to my remembrance. His Word was flowing like a river in my soul. He said:

> *Ye are of God little children, and have overcome them: because greater is He that is in you than he that is in the world.*
> (I John 4:4)

> *No weapon that is formed against you shall prosper; and every tongue that shall rise against thee in judgment thou shalt condemn. This is the heritage of the servants of the Lord, and their righteousness is of me, saith the Lord.* (Isaiah 54:17)

> *For God hath not given us the spirit of fear; but of power and of love and of a sound mind.* (II Timothy 1:7)

I CAN NOT DOUBT

God would talk to me through His Word, and I would respond by saying "I can not doubt. I cannot waver. Lord, I believe what You said."

When I visited with my son in the jail, my first words to him were about what God said:

> *If we confess our sins He is faithful and just to forgive us our sins and to cleanse us from all unrighteousness.* (I John 1:9)

I asked him if he believed that. He said yes. I asked him what happened, and he told me. My response was "That is not murder! It's not that you intended or planned to do this." I tried to encourage him, but it was hard. He asked me to leave my Bible with him. I said I would bring it to him in the morning.

I mentioned to my son that a woman had called me. He said she was the girl he had been seeing and it was her brother that got killed. I told him she offered me a place to stay. He said I would be all right with her. I was doubtful, but I trusted him because I didn't know anyone there. So, I called her and she came to pick me up from the jail.

She and I talked most of the night. She said her family was upset with her for inviting me to stay with her, but she wanted to stand by my son. She said, "He didn't want to fight my brother, and he was trying to leave. As he was going out the door my brother hit him in the head from behind. I hollered to my brother to stop and just let him leave, but he wouldn't. So they were fighting. I called the police." She explained how my son had a paring knife in his pocket he used to peel apples while at work. He pulled it out in hopes that if the man saw he had a weapon, he would back off. But he didn't. When the man lunged to hit him again, the knife caught him in the chest. My son tried to help him until the paramedics came. But he died at the hospital. I thanked her for being honest with me because I knew that it had to be difficult because her brother lost his life.

THE FUNERAL

The funeral was the next day. She wanted me to go. I told her I would go, but I didn't want to ride with her for the sake of appearances. My son had given me the names and telephone numbers of some of his Marine buddies to call if I needed anything. I called and someone came to take me to the funeral.

I went to the funeral, not so much as out of respect, but because I wanted to view the size of the body of the man. My son is solid, but small. When I went up to the front of the church to view the body, that's when I heard someone point me out. "That's the mother of the Marine who killed him."

The remarks really made me uncomfortable, and I knew it was a mistake for me to be there. But, I was there. I wasn't afraid of any possible trouble, because I had two military police with me.

What I was not prepared for was more upsetting to me. The minister ended the service and walked to the back of the church. There was a small vestibule. He made the committal remarks, and everyone started leaving, family first. Then, I heard screaming, hollering and crying. It made me sit back down. I didn't know what was happening. When it came time for my row to leave, then I saw what was going on. They had re-opened the casket at the front door as people were leaving the church for a last viewing. I was horrified, because they don't do that in Detroit. So I was not prepared for that. It was awful. I wouldn't exit of the church through the front entrance. I asked a nurse if there was another door. I couldn't face that family again behind that. So, I left through the side door. I told my two Marines that I needed somewhere else to stay for the night. They said, "No problem. We'll take you to pick up your things and take you to somewhere you will feel safe." They took me to my son's Gunnery Sergeant's home. I had to stay in Jacksonville another night.

I went to see my son the next morning and took him my Bible. I told him, "Hold on and believe God. God is merciful and gracious. His mercy is from everlasting to everlasting. And, He is going to bring us through this."

I had gone to speak with my son's attorney while I was there. The charge was first-degree murder. I told him I listened to my son and what he described to me is not murder. He agreed, but those were the charges. He advised me that his bail was set at $100,000.00. He wanted to know if I owned any property that I could put up as security. He explained the process to me. I told him I didn't have that kind of money and didn't know if I could get it. He said my son would have to stay in jail until he went to trial, and that he wanted to try to avoid that. I agreed to keep in touch with him.

THE SUPPORT OF MY FAMILY

When I returned home to Detroit, I went to see my uncle. He wears two hats, uncle and pastor. That day he was uncle. I told him what the bond was and asked if he could help me. He said he would discuss it with his wife and get back to me. He advised me to see how much of the bond I could come up with.

When he got back to me, he had devised a plan. My uncle is sort of the head of the family. Everyone looks up to him. He called a family meeting and asked all the heads of each family to loan him a certain amount of money. He would be responsible for collecting the money back from me.

The Lord had given him a workable plan, and most importantly, my family helped me in my greatest time of financial need. We made the bail after a couple of months. I will always appreciate my mother, two sisters, aunts, uncles and cousins for their support of me and my children.

God has always carried me through the storms of life. God is the strength of my life. God is so merciful; and, He always makes a way when I don't see my way. He put a determination within me to survive. I went through hell on more than one occasion, but He brought me out. I was crying and praying, but He was right there upholding me.

EVERYTHING IS IN THE BOOK

Then one night, I remembered what my grandfather told me. He said, "Cheryl, everything concerning life is in the book [the Bible]." Pastor Anderson is always quoting this Scripture:

> *According as his divine power hath given unto us all things that pertain unto life and godliness through the knowledge of him that hath called us to glory and virtue.* (II Peter 1:3)

I started searching the concordance for the word *manslaughter.* I couldn't find it. Since they had charged him with first-degree murder I looked up the word *murder.* Believe it or not, God had given me His Word that He would bring my son out.

> *And the Lord spoke unto Moses, saying speak unto the children of Israel, and say unto them, when ye be come over Jordan into the land of Canaan; Then ye shall appoint you cities to be cities of refuge for you; that the slayer may flee thither, which killeth any person at unawares (*meaning unintentionally*). And they shall be unto you cities for refuge from the avenger; that the manslayer die not, until he stand before the congregation in judgment.* (Numbers 35:9-12)

I read that Scripture over and over that night. My grandfather was right. Everything is in the book. More importantly, God had imparted an unwavering faith in me. I couldn't wait to tell my pastor what God had shown me. His response was not what I expected. I was excited. I was overjoyed. But, he didn't get excited with me. He said, "Well, if you believe that's what God told you, I'm going to just believe with you." But, there was no enthusiasm. I was hurt, and I lashed out at him, "You told me that God is greater than any problem. You told me when Daniel was in the lion's den, that God shut the lion's mouth. You told me when the three Hebrew boys were thrown in the fiery furnace, Jesus stepped in with them. You told me God is the same, yesterday, today and forever. You told me, when Peter and Paul and the other disciples were put in prison, God brought them out. That's what you told me. And I believed you." His response was "Lord, help my unbelief." I left.

One of my aunts said to me, "Cheryl that boy is strong and he can do ten years easy. He will still be a young man when he gets out." I responded, "I'm not going to talk to any of you anymore until this thing is over. Because if you don't believe like I believe, I'm not going to talk to anyone that doubts that God can do it."

I BELIEVED GOD

I cried and I cried. I prayed and cried. I continued to shout (dance) and praise the God of my salvation. I kept telling my mother that this is all I know to do. This is what I've been taught: In everything, give thanks. God didn't say for everything. But, while you're in the storm, praise Him anyway. That's what the pastor taught us. So, that was all I knew to do because I believed his report. But more importantly, I believed God.

One Saturday, I went to visit my mother. I told her what Jesus said:

> *And whatsoever ye shall ask in my name, that will I do, that the Father may be glorified in the Son. If ye shall ask any thing in my name, I will do it.* (John 14:13-14)

He said that if I asked and doubted not, He would do it. He said:

> *But let him ask in faith, nothing wavering. For he that wavereth is like a wave of the sea driven with the wind and tossed. For let not that man think that he shall receive any thing of the Lord. A double-minded man is unstable in all his ways.* (James 1:6-8)

I said, "Mama, I can't waver and I can't doubt. I believe God. I have to hold on to what He said."

> *God is not a man that He should lie neither the son of man that He should repent: hath he said, and shall he not do it? Or hath he spoken, and shall he not make it good?* (Numbers 23:19)

"Mama, all I got is His Word and I'm going to stand on it." She said, "Baby, you stand on it then and don't pay them any attention. They believe it, but he is not their son. So, they can't feel what you feel." My stepfather had been listening to our conversation. He came in and said, "Baby, I wouldn't go to church as much as you do and not believe what God said." They encouraged me. And, I was glad my mother knew I was not going to lose my mind.

It was a long seven months. I had told my Jurisdictional Supervisor what was happening because I was very active in the jurisdiction and she was a praying woman. I was missing a lot of meetings working so much overtime to help make his bail.

God is so good! He fixed it so that they let my son come home for a week. Can you believe that–A person charged with first-degree murder leaving the state? But, the Marines put him on a plane from North Carolina to Detroit. I tell you, God is a wonder! Both my son's attorney, who was a public defender and the prosecuting attorney came to Detroit to take depositions. My son had given them the names of all the people he knew would vouch for his character. Detroit was his home. I contacted his school counselor, his baseball coach, Pastor Anderson and three or four neighbors. They were all willing to give depositions. So, we set it up to be held at my home and the church.

IF YOU HAVE JUST A LITTLE

The trial date came up in August. My son called me to make sure I was coming. I told him yes. He told me that he felt his life was hanging in the balance; that everything he had worked for appeared to be going down the drain. I said to him, "Baby, I got enough faith to believe God is going to bring you out. All I need you to do is believe with me."

> *And Jesus said unto them, because of your unbelief: for verily I say unto you, if ye have faith as a grain of mustard seed, ye shall say unto this mountain, remove hence to yonder place; and it shall remove; and nothing shall be impossible unto you.*
>
> (Matthew 17:20)

"If you have just a little, I got enough to go through. Do you believe what I said about God?" He answered, "Yes Mama." I assured him it would be all right. I called it skirt tail faith.

The trial lasted three days. I was the last person to testify. It went to the jury on the second day, and the jury was hung. My son was devastated. I reminded him of what Pastor Anderson said, "When they try gold, they put it in the fire. And, they turn the heat up. So hold on, God is going to do what He said."

I called my Jurisdictional Supervisor at five o'clock in the morning and told her the jury was hung. She just answered, "The devil is a liar and he is going to un-hang that jury." She prayed for and encouraged me so much. The next day, it was over. The jury said "Not guilty!" That's when I broke down. I sat there with my head in my hands crying. I didn't realize everyone had left the courtroom. I was just sitting there. Everyone was outside talking to the media.

My son came back in the courtroom to get me, "Come on Ma. Let's go home. The Marines have given me leave." We left the courthouse and went to the base. His friends wanted to celebrate with him. But, he said he was going home for a few days and they could celebrate when he got back. He threw some things in his duffle bag and we hit the highway.

Faith moves mountains because God is faithful to His Word!

I thought this was the hardest trial I would ever have to endure, but it wasn't.

Faith in Due Season

2

On May 29, 1997, I went to visit my dad on his birthday. I walked upon his porch and started to ring the doorbell. I remember it well. He pulled up in the driveway, higher than a Georgia Pine—as they say. He was drunk. I stood there, asking, "Lord, is this all there is going to be to my life? Is my whole life just supposed to be about struggling and taking care of people that are not even trying to serve you? When is my time?" He amazes me when He answers right away. Most times, I have to wait for an answer. He put in my spirit, "Your time is now." I replied. "Lord, if you show me what to do, I'm gone."

The Lord worked in my mind that I could pull my funds from my 401K and go to California to visit my son. I called my son that night and asked if I could come and visit him for about four months. He had been stationed in Okinawa for three years. We had not really spent any quality time together since he joined the Marines in 1986. He welcomed me.

I went into work that following Monday and typed my resignation. I could hardly believe the response I got. A couple hours later, my manager pulled me into a conference room to find out what was wrong. I said, "Nothing. I'm going to retire. This has nothing to do with anyone but me. No one has done anything to me. I don't have a problem with work. I just need to enjoy part of my life. I sense that now is the time to do it." I gave a two-month notice because I knew they would need me to train some people. I had worked in Farmington Hills for eleven and a half years. My manager was shocked, but all he could say was OK.

THE NEXT TRIAL

One day, while I was at work, I felt sharp pains in my breasts. It was terrible. I said, "Devil, you are a liar. I'm going to California." I folded my arms across my breasts and prayed to God to stop the pain. "Lord, please don't let this be happening to me now." I called my doctor and made an appointment. When I went to the doctor I said to him, "I have given my resignation and I'm going to retire the end of June. So whatever you need to do, you have to do it by then because I'm leaving for California." He agreed.

He questioned when was the last time I had a mammogram? I told him a year ago. He then ordered a new one. He scheduled at Grace Hospital that same week for the mammogram. The nurse came back and informed me I had had a mammogram about six months prior and not a year ago. But, it was good that I'd taken another one because she saw some abnormalities.

They sent my x-ray results to the doctor. When he reviewed them, he wanted me to see a surgeon and have a biopsy. I agreed, but reminded him that I would be leaving at the end of June and my insurance would be cancelled. He said he understood. The hospital scheduled the biopsy. I asked my pastor to pray for me.

I had an appointment to see the surgeon to get the results. I worked most of the day and went to see him at three o'clock. When I got to his office, he said, "I have been waiting for you all day. I had seven patients scheduled today, and you were the only one I had good news for. You don't have cancer." I said, "Thank You Lord!" I tell you, God is so good. I never get tired of thanking Him. I never get tired of saying how good He is! He truly is a wonder in my soul!

I called my benefits representative to submit the paperwork to withdraw the funds from my 401K. The representative questioned why I was withdrawing everything. I explained it to him. He suggested taking out a loan. I told him that I didn't need a loan. He politely said, "Your check would be in the mail. You should receive it in about two weeks."

Then, I started telling my other four children and my family that I was going to retire and go visit my oldest son in California. Their response was why so long? My mother and sister's response was, "That's foolishness. Why would you quit your job at almost fifty? Where are you going to find another job at your age?" They said so many negative things. But, it didn't matter to me. The Lord had said it was my time, and I was going. Now, don't think for a moment that I wasn't scared. I was. But, I was going anyway.

THE YEAR OF JUBILEE

Pastor Anderson was teaching that Friday night on the Year of Jubilee from Leviticus 25. He is such a profound teacher. When service was concluded, I said to him, "Pastor, I'm going into my year of Jubilee." He just smiled and looked at me. I do know how to rightly divide the word of truth. So I know that was just for the children of Israel. But, God put everything in His Word so we can see what He did for His chosen people; so that we could have the assurance that He will do the same for us.

I needed some rest from my labor and He was going to provide. I was headed into my due season. No one in my family really understood. But, it was OK, as long as I understood. I knew God was speaking to me in my spirit; and, the Holy Ghost was giving me directions. This was my season and I was not going to miss it.

Now, I had time on my hands. I had prayed and asked God to allow me to see just a little of His beauty before I leave this world. So, I told my son I was coming on the bus so that I could see the country. This is a beautiful country. I never had anyone to travel with or take me anywhere. God had provided a way. He is so good. He is so gracious and kind. He is full of compassion.

My son knew he needed to find a church for me to attend, not just the chapel on base. When I arrived on Saturday, I told him I would rest from the long bus ride. I looked in the Yellow Pages and found one Church of God in Christ in Santa Ana.

GOSPEL LIGHT CHURCH

I knew I could go to church the following Sunday. However, my son told me that his friends went to church and they invited him to bring me. It was the same one that I had found in the Yellow Pages. That was my first time attending Gospel Light Church. After the service, I introduced myself to the pastor and told him I was an evangelist, visiting from Detroit. He said, "Before you leave, I want you to speak for us." I said to myself, "Thank You, Lord."

Gospel Light was multi-cultural and the pastor had a wonderful teaching ministry. He was not a "hooper". The pastor had given me a date to speak. So, I had been fasting and praying. The Lord gave me a message entitled, "Lord, Break the Curse and Bring Deliverance to this House." The Spirit of God moved in a powerful way.

Having entered the Marine Corp before I started ministering, this was my son's first time hearing me speaking publicly. He came up to me, in tears, and hugged me so tightly. He said, "Mama, you preach like Uncle Clemmon." I took that as a wonderful compliment to Pastor Anderson. It meant he had taught me well.

After that service, the pastor asked me if I could speak again that evening for the Mother's Board service. I had to pray, "Lord, give me what to say." He did. I had a heart to heart, motherly talk with the saints.

A PRAYING MOTHER

I was faithful in my attendance to Gospel Light Church while I was visiting with my son. I loved Sunday school and Bible study. Most importantly, I love eight o'clock prayer. A long time ago, I asked the Lord to make me a praying mother. He did! That's the only way I knew how to raise my children. I prayed, everyday, for the Lord to save my children. That's what I had heard my grandmother do for her eleven. It's the only thing that has brought me through life's struggles.

I always like to get to church in time for the beginning prayer. It sets the tone for the rest of my Sunday. Prayer is the key!

> *Thus saith the Lord of hosts, consider ye and call for the mourning women, that they may come; and send for the cunning*

women that they may come: And let them make haste, and take up a wailing for us, that our eyes may run down with tears, and our eyelids gush out with waters. (Jeremiah 9:17-18)

PREPARING FOR THE BLESSING

While I was in California, I had a dream. Since I don't dream often, I call it my 1997 dream.

> *The prophet that hath a dream let him tell a dream; and he that hath my word, let him speak my word faithfully.*
> (Jeremiah 23:28a)

The Lord put in my spirit, "I'm going to prepare you for the blessing that I have prepared for you." From that point I started living with an expectation that God was going to give me the desires of my heart. One of which is to experience married life the way He had intended. I never had that expectation before, especially since I have been divorced for over thirty years.

I believe God will allow whomever He has prepared for me to find me…once He has completed preparing me. God instructed me to just delight myself in Him. Those were the most wonderful four months I had ever had in my life.

Then, I got a telephone call from my mother saying Pastor Anderson was sick. I told my son I've got to go home. I called Pastor Anderson to talk with him. He could barely talk above a whisper because he was so weak. But, he knew my voice. I told him to hold on. God is going to bring him through. I asked him not to give up.

I have to interject this. We, the saints, do not really know and understand how much we take from the men and women of God. It is so important to pray for our leaders. We must speak life back into them and encourage them. They give out of themselves until sometimes they have no reserve. As the people of God, we must learn how to put something back so they too can live.

So; I went back home to Detroit.

The funniest thing happened. I called some friends at my old job when I got home. They told the managers I was back. One of the vice-presidents called me and asked if I was coming back to work. I questioned, "You want me to come back to work there?" Her reply was, "Yes. We need you." So, I went back to work for the same company. God is so good. He provides and makes ways when you can't see your way.

Moving Forward Faith

3

In the month of May, the Lord impressed upon me to call California and pray for my son's friend. I don't know why, but I did. They were glad that I had called. I told his wife that I needed to pray for her husband. She received it and handed her husband the phone. I told him, "I don't know what is going on, but the Lord said for me to call and pray for you." He accepted and time went on.

In June 1998, the Lord put a sense of urgency in my spirit to return to California. I questioned Him about it over and over again. He said, "You have to go into the land to inherit the promise." Let me tell you, there is a place of blessings, and it is in our obedience to Him. I was not so sure this time that it was the Lord speaking to me because I had not asked God about moving. So, my question was "Lord is this you talking to me?" He said, "Be strong and of a good courage."

I almost couldn't believe I was having this dialogue with the Lord in my mind. I kept on questioning. "Lord, are You sure You are telling me to go? Is this really You, Lord, or is it someone else? Is this my imagination working overtime?"

However, the urgency was there. I needed to be in California by year-end. I was crying and praying now because I knew my son was leaving California, coming to Detroit for recruiting duty. I did not understand the purpose for God telling me to go. For every question, God gave me an answer. His Word would come to me. I asked, "Lord where am I going to stay? How am I going to live?" He said:

> *Be careful for nothing; but in every thing by prayer and supplication with thanksgiving let your requests be made known unto God.* (Philippians 4:6)

> *Therefore I say unto you, take no thought for your life, what ye shall eat, or what ye shall drink; nor yet for your body, what ye shall put on. Is not the life more than meat, and the body than raiment? Behold the fowls of the air: for they sow not, neither do they reap, nor gather into barns; yet your heavenly Father feedeth them. Are ye not much better than they? And why take ye thought for raiment? Consider the lilies of the field, how they grow; they toil not, neither do they spin.* (Matthew 6:25-26, 28)

"Lord," I said, "all of my family is here." He said:

> *If, any man come to me and hate not his father, and mother, and wife and children, and brethren and sisters, yea, and his own life also, he cannot be my disciple.* (Luke 14:26)

This was serious stuff! This was really happening to me. I was scared. He responded with His Word.

> *For God hath not given us the spirit of fear but of power, and of love, and of a sound mind.* (II Timothy 1:7)

He kept showing me Joshua. I would hear His instructions to Joshua over and over in my spirit.

> *Have not I commanded thee? Be strong and of a good courage; be not afraid, neither be thou dismayed: for the Lord thy God is with thee whithersoever thou goest.* (Joshua 1:9)

"YES, LORD!"

I prayed and cried. Finally, I said "Yes, Lord!" And, once I did, the struggle of my decision left me. I told my family that I was going back to California. They wanted to know why. I said, "I don't know. I just know I'm going because the Lord said, 'Go.' He has put a sense of urgency in my spirit, but He has not shown me His purpose. I don't have a sense of death, but I have a sense of urgency to be there. I have to be there by the end of the year."

I really had a hard time leaving my youngest daughter. She was twenty-four years old, but she was my baby. She never knew her dad because he passed away when she was three years old. So, to leave her was very hard. I really had to pray about this thing. But she surprised me. She said, "Mama I understand. You have got to go tell your story." I'm crying just writing this. This is so overwhelming to me.

It was also hard to leave my dad because he depended on me. I was the only child he had that would go see about him. I knew my oldest sister was going to look after my mother and my younger sister but my dad didn't have anyone but me…and I love him so. But, I had to tell him I was leaving. He wanted to know when I would be coming back. I said, "I don't know. The Lord said for me to go for a season and I don't know how long that is."

My oldest daughter was living in Camden, New Jersey with her husband and children. She called and asked, "Mama, would you come and get me?" I was shocked. I questioned what was going on. She had left Detroit a few months after graduating high school and had been gone about ten years. I asked was she serious because I was leaving for California. She said yes, and the situation was serious. She was scared. I told her I would call her brothers and make arrangements to come get her. I told her I couldn't get there until the first weekend in October. She felt she could hold on until then.

I called my son's friends in California. I asked to speak to the woman of the house. I told her the Lord had instructed me to come back to California and I needed a place to stay until I could get on my feet. They both received me, with open arms. I told her I would be mailing my study books; and that I would bring my clothes with me. We had an agreement.

The night I emptied my last dresser drawer with my things, I was so overwhelmed. I couldn't stop crying. I fell back on my bed and cried, "Lord I don't have another dresser to call my own to put my clothes in." I mean I was overwhelmed. My closet was empty. Everything was packed. I was leaving my house of twenty-two years. I was leaving my family and my friends. I was going to California, with a sense of urgency–for a purpose I did not know.

My middle daughter came to see me. She was hurting badly. She wanted to know if she was the reason I was leaving. "No," I said, "God told me to go, so I'm going." My grandmother used to say, sing with an understanding. I try to do that. And I have stopped singing the song, I'll Go. I'm learning more and more God will hold you to whatever you say or sing.

I made it to California December 31, 1998. I stayed on the military base with my friends. They call me Mother. They had prepared a room for me, and said don't worry about anything. They had to adjust to my praying at five o'clock every morning, but they didn't mind. After about a week, I started taking them to work so I could learn how to drive around the Cities of Tustin and Santa Ana.

MY LESSONS

We attended Gospel Light Church, and I advised the pastor I wanted to be under watch-care. I remember asking God to teach me what it means to be an evangelist. I guess my lessons were starting. He put in my spirit there has to be a time of observation, a time of work and a time of training someone else how to do whatever it is I do. So, I did not try to get involved right away. I attended the eight o'clock prayer and Sunday school. I really had to seek God for the purpose. The pastor asked me why was I there and I told him I didn't know. I explained that God didn't tell me His purpose.

Then, the Lord started revealing things to me. He started showing me things that I had never seen before in my life. I said, "Lord, You have thrown me out here with the wolves." I got scared and almost ran back home. But the Lord said, "Don't run. I have you covered. Keep your eyes open and don't let your feet run into mischief."

The church had a large bulletin board, and the pastor asked me if I could do something with it. So I started decorating the bulletin board. I would change the background color and Scripture themes every month. I began to teach Sunday School. I was starting to get involved in the church. But I needed a job so that I could get an apartment. I was praying and talking to people, but the people were not really responsive. No one seemed to know anything about the temp agencies.

One Sunday, a visitor came up to me after service and said, "The Lord told me that you needed a job. Come to my job and I'll help you find a job. Here's my card and the directions." It was a resource center in Santa Ana. I started going there everyday and sending out my resume. But, I never saw the woman who had given me the card.

THE PURPOSE

Remember the husband I prayed for in May? It was almost the end of January 1999 when he said to me, "Mother, I'm part of the purpose you came here." He explained to me his situation. When I had called him the previous May, he knew it was the Lord trying to warn him. But, things happened. Anyway, they got through that. But, it was a very difficult time for him and his wife. I quoted something to him I had read, "Faith, knocking on mercy's door, never goes unanswered." The Lord had sent me to be there for those young people. I thank Him for allowing me to touch their lives and for them touching mine. Now, he was gone away for a while and his wife and I had to make it without him.

I still didn't have a job. I prayed, "Lord, if You don't open up a door, I'm going to take that to mean the season is over and I'm going to go back home." The Lord opened up a door at a large insurance company in Irvine. It paid a lot more than ten dollars an hour. I thanked the Lord and figured that meant the season isn't over.

Again, I went to the Lord, "My friend has to leave me and move down to Oceanside. I don't have transportation and I don't know anything about the buses here. I need a car." The Holy Ghost put in my spirit to call my credit union. I responded, "For what? I've only been working a week and a half (eight days)." He said, "Call your credit union?" I said, "That doesn't make any sense. I have only been in California three months."

He said, "Call your credit union." So I did. I called on a Wednesday. That Friday, they called me back and said, "Ms. Black, do you want us to mail your check or do you want to come in and pick it up?" I picked it up. I told God thank you. And, again I figured the season wasn't over. On that Saturday, I had a new car. God was moving.

When I got to work on Monday, I was told Friday would be my last day. I didn't even get upset. I went to lunch and I told the Lord that this is His problem. I said, "I know you didn't bring me out here to make me homeless and put me in debt. So, since You are in charge, You have to handle this. I'm not going to worry about it because I did not create this situation." And, I meant that. I know God was having mercy because He let me live through that conversation.

I went to church and told the pastor I wouldn't have a job as of Friday. He questioned what I was going to do. "Nothing," I said, "This is God's problem. He has created it, so He has to fix it. I believe God sent me here for His purpose. And, I'm just here on His Word." The pastor looked at me like I was crazy.

The next Tuesday I went for another interview at another large insurance company in Newport Beach. On Wednesday I started work. I worked as a temp for a year and then I was hired as a permanent employee. I keep on saying that God is a wonder. He truly is. And, of course I said, "Lord, I guess the season isn't over."

HIDE ME IN THE SECRET PLACE

There was trouble and a lot of strife at the church. I worked really hard at Gospel Light for a little over two years. The Lord had sent me there for a purpose that I didn't know or understand. But, He did reveal it on a need to know basis. Not only did He reveal it to me, but he revealed it to those around me, especially the pastor. I shared some things with the pastor and some things I couldn't. However, I had done what the Lord sent me there to do. And, believe me, it was more than doing a bulletin board.

I had received a warning in my spirit that it was time for me to go. But, I didn't know where to go. I didn't know any other churches or how to get up to Los Angeles well enough to find another church. Things were starting to get ugly. A struggle was going on for me to stay, but the spirit of God said for me to leave. I was crying and praying again. I prayed to the Lord, "I need You to hide me in the secret place of Your pavilion."

A PLACE OF REFUGE

My roommate announced that she was getting married. I was surprised. But I said, "OK. I'll move as soon as I get back from visiting my dad." When I got ready to leave my dad, again it was really hard because his health was declining. I prayed, "If You want me to stay in California, I need to have a sense of family." I needed people that didn't act like everything was all about Hollywood–normal people that didn't put on airs; people I could just call and talk to without fear of gossip. I needed a mother here too. So, He provided that for me. He has put some very special people in my life to be my family away from home. And, I love them all.

I called my friends, who had moved down to Oceanside, and told them I needed a place to stay. They made room for me. And, just like that, God pulled me away from what was becoming a stressful and hostile situation for me.

Then, the organist left and started his own church in a hotel. I started driving up from Oceanside to attend the services. The Lord blessed and He started healing the hurt. He also started moving in me in a way that I had never experienced. The praise and worship service would be going on, and I would just melt in His presence. I started lying on the floor in total submission and worship to the God of my salvation. It just happened. His presence was overwhelming me. Sometimes, I could not stand in the presence of the Lord. I would be singing one minute, kneeling down one minute and lying down the next.

It was strange and it was awesome. I wasn't concerned about what anyone thought. It didn't matter what I was wearing. All I knew was God was doing something in me. I always ask the Lord to take out of me whatever is not pleasing to Him, and put in me those things that He wants and need me to have. This went on for about seven or eight months.

Sustaining Faith

4

Then it happened. January 2002, I received another horrible telephone call. My youngest son was in jail in Sapulpa, Oklahoma. I wasn't even sure where Oklahoma was. And, I surely had not heard of Sapulpa. I asked him, "What are you doing in Oklahoma in jail?" He kept saying, "Ma, I can't give you any details. I just need you to help me get out of here. Call my wife. She'll be able to tell you something."

I became a nervous wreck. I went to a payphone to call a friend. I needed someone to pray for me. I really couldn't pray right then. And, I needed to talk to somebody. We talked and he prayed for me. I stayed at work as long as I could handle it. But, my emotions starting welling up on the inside; I couldn't hold it any longer. I told my supervisor I had to leave. I barely made it out the building before the tears started flowing. I felt like screaming, but I couldn't do that. I felt like letting everything go, but I couldn't do that.

I was driving down Jamboree and the Lord spoke to me: "Don't worry Cheryl. I have you and your son in My hands. Trust Me." I said, "I trust You, Lord, with my life and the lives of my children.

But, this is so hard. How am I supposed to handle this? I don't have the same support system I had back home. I don't have any blood family here." He just kept telling me to trust Him.

I made it home, put my face in my pillow and screamed. I screamed as long as I wanted to. I needed the pain to go away. Any mother who has experienced this kind of situation knows you almost cannot bear the pain. I cried and I cried. I knew I needed to stop crying before I made myself sick. But, I couldn't. This is it! This is the hardest of all my trials. I felt so completely helpless. I knew I had absolutely no control over what was going on in my son's life.

My son called me at home. He gave me the name of a bondman and told me what it was going to take to get him out of jail. He wanted me to sign over my house for security. I was hurting and he was talking fast. I was listening and trying not to cry. He was telling me, "Ma, don't cry. I can't take it when you cry. And, I can't be crying in here. So, please stop crying."

I questioned, "Why do you need my house? Why can't the people you were dealing with get you out of jail? What are the charges? You have got to tell me something more than 'Ma, I need you to get me out of here.'" He was begging me to help him. He was pulling my heart out. He was losing it. He asked me if I wanted him to stay there. I said, "No, but I didn't put you in there." He said, "Ma, I can't stay in here."

THE PRESSURE WAS ENORMOUS

I was hurting so badly. The pain felt like someone had put a knife in my heart. My son had never been disrespectful to me in his life. However, there were times when I was hearing a stranger. He was pleading with me one minute, talking to me like I was stupid the next. I said, "Wait a minute. Do you know who you are talking to?"

My friend called to check on me. I thank God for placing some people in my path that could pray for me when I needed it. It was horrible. My son was calling me everyday, asking me to help him. I was not sleeping. And, I still had to get up and go to work. The pressure was enormous. The stress of this situation was heavy–almost unbearable. But, God just kept saying, "Trust Me, Cheryl." And, I just kept responding, "I trust You Lord."

"I don't want to lose my house," I told my son. "If I lose my house, your sister and her family would be in the streets. I want to help you but I can't." He said, "I'm not going to let you lose your house." I told him, "You are not in control. God is in control." He told me that I couldn't take my house to Heaven. "No," I answered. "I cannot take my house to Heaven. But, I can take you."

A week passed. He was calling and I was crying. I was praying and crying. I kept telling God that this is too hard. He would simply put in my spirit to trust Him. I would respond, "I trust You, Lord. But, how do I get through this?" He reminded me of when my youngest aunt passed away. Two months after that, one of my older aunts lost her husband. Two months after that, the same aunt lost another one of her sons. She never missed a Sunday from church. She would come. She would cry. But, she never stopped going to church. Whenever she would cry, we all would be crying with her. But, she never stopped going. She never stopped praising God. If all she could do was sit through the service, she was there. The Lord strengthened her, day by day, Sunday by Sunday.

I stopped thinking ahead and asked God to just give me strength, day by day. I walked around the building at work, everyday, asking Him to give me more strength. I asked Him to help me! "I'm standing in the strength of Your Word," I would declare.

No one has ever had to beg me for anything, especially not my children. My son is a barber. He is the son that likes to take me to Sunday brunch and out to dinner. He made sure I had a mother's ring. He has always done nice things for me. But, he made a wrong turn in his life.

I remember coming home from church one Sunday, and found him pacing the kitchen floor. I asked him what was wrong. He told me he felt like he was going under. He needed to quit his job, because he needed to get away from some people. I told him, "Quit. The Lord will open up another door. But, you don't have to get involved in drugs to make money. You are blessed with a gift to cut hair." So, he quit that job. He started working in another barbershop. But, he tried to hold on to the same friends. I warned him, over and over again. I would tell him that he needed to get off the devil's territory, because he doesn't play fair.

> *The thief cometh not, but for to steal, kill and destroy: I am come that they might have life, and that they might have it more abundantly.* (John 10:10)

God was merciful to him, time and time again.

THE LORD WAS HOLDING ME

Then, the Lord revealed another part of His purpose for sending me to California. He said to me, "Cheryl, your prayer to Me everyday is, 'Lord save my children.' You did not remarry for over thirty years because you were afraid that someone might abuse your children. But whom I love, I chasten. So, I had to move you out of My way so that I could draw them to myself. You could not bear to watch it. But, they have to learn how to depend on Me, not you. You can not save them. They have to learn how to pray for themselves. They have to learn to call on Me. They have to develop a personal relationship with Me. They need to recognize that they need Me, more than they need you." I finally stopped asking God if the season is over. I stopped asking God if I could go back home. The Lord was holding me.

The Holy Ghost quickened the evangelist spirit in me. He reminded me who I was. Mama Cheryl had to go sit down because all she was doing was crying and fussing. She was not ministering. And, my children know when mama is talking or when Missionary Black is talking. They know how to tune mama out. But, they listen, attentively, when the missionary is speaking. I told my son what the Lord said:

> *Give not that which is holy unto the dogs, neither cast ye your pearls before swine, lest they trample them under their feet, and turn again and rend you.* (Matthew 7:6)

My strength was coming up and out. I told him, "I prayed for a decent place to raise my children. God provided for me to get that house and I am not going to lose it. God has already been so very merciful to you. Now, this thing is between you and God. And, there is really nothing I can do. Since you've stopped listening to everyone who loves and cares about you, God stepped in. God had to arrest you and sit you down so that you could do nothing but listen to Him. I remind you,

> *Good understanding giveth favour: but the way of transgressors is hard.* (Proverbs 13:15)"

He still wasn't ready to hear that. His anger was starting to come out. He said, "If it had been my brother, you would have helped him. Your family had helped raise bail money for my brother. Although the circumstances are different, I am your son, too."

"The circumstances make the difference," I told him. "The majority of my aunts and uncles are older now, and they are retired. You chose to do whatever you have done. Now, you have to suffer the consequences of your actions. I have always said that God is a God of love. He is kind and full of compassion. But, He is also a God of wrath and judgment. God has been merciful to you, over and over again. God said,

> *If we confess our sins, He is faithful and just to forgive us our sins, and to cleanse us from all unrighteousness.* (I John 1:9)

God is being merciful to you, even now, because you're still living."

TOUGH LOVE

We went through some really rough times. My son was saying a lot of hurtful things. But, he would always say he was not trying to disrespect me. He was just expressing how he felt.

Days had passed, now weeks were passing. It was still difficult, and I was still praying and crying everyday. I wanted the crying to stop.

My friend, who was like a mother to me, said, "It's OK to cry. Cry until you're empty." The burden was so heavy. The Lord reminded me:

> *Casting all your care upon him; for he careth for you.*
> (I Peter 5:7)

I said, "Lord, You have to take this burden, then. It is too heavy for me. I gave it to Him. I truly did. I'm still in California because the Lord sent me here for His purpose. And, my son is still in jail. The Lord has lifted me because I say to Him, "You are my strength.

You are my peace. You are my provider and my protection. Lord, I'm out here on Your Word."

Weeks have turned into months. The pain has subsided. It comes and it goes. Though I'm still going through this trial with my son, God is still moving. And, I know He is going to bring us out. I don't cry as much now or as often. I am reminded that the joy of the Lord is my strength.

Faith in the Storm

5

Things are happening really fast in my life right now. So, I have to note every important date. In March, something wonderfully strange happened to me. I had gone to church early for prayer, as I always do. This time, the Spirit had me walking up and down the front of the church before the start of services. The praise and worship ushered in the presence of God. I ended up lying on the floor again.

Then, suddenly, I got up off the floor and started running through the church, touching people. I could hardly see because I was so drunk in the Spirit. He was moving me so fast. And, I wasn't really stopping to watch for any results. I was just moving. However, I did see one young man fall back in his seat. Then, I realized another young man in the choir had kneeled down. So, I went up to the choir and touched them. The Lord moved in that church that day. I was so exhausted; I barely had strength to drive home.

We had a singing engagement at a retirement home. I pressed my way and went. When I saw the pastor, I asked him to pray for me.

He said, "Oh, nice moves!" I was almost floored. I was shocked at his response and hurt.

The following Sunday, the Lord moved again but not exactly the same way. The Spirit did lead me to lay my hands on a couple of people and He blessed them. The Spirit of God started manifesting Himself in and through me.

The pastor could not discern how to give me instruction. So, he just rebuked me openly–even though the people were blessed. It grieved my spirit. I didn't know what to do. The pastor wouldn't talk to me. And, since I knew there were other issues going on at the church, I knew it was time for me to leave. I had to leave because I would not be allowed to operate freely in this new gift. God was moving in me. And, I needed my spirit to be free to allow the Holy Spirit to move through me. I needed freedom to bless His people, in whatever manner He chose. I could not hold Him in and grieve the Holy Ghost.

I NEEDED STABILITY

I prayed and I cried. I wanted and needed to be settled. I needed stability and a sense of belonging. I needed a church home. I had had one pastor for most of my entire life. Now, I was moving from here to there. I felt like I was floundering around. I prayed for God to give me understanding and direction.

I was moved to write to Bishop Noel Jones, though I had never met him. I needed someone in California in authority to know I was out here "on the field" as they call it. And, I was in trouble. Bishops oversee Elders. I had attended Greater Bethany with a friend once before. So, I asked her for the address and directions to the church. I felt like I was without a covering. Sheep need a shepherd. I had to be watching, fasting, and praying because I still did not have an under shepherd to protect and shield me. And that was not good.

Pastor Anderson loved to quote, "No man is an island. No man stands alone. Each man's joy is joy to me. Each man's sorrow is my own." Pastor Anderson had taught me for over thirty-four years. The message he preached that drew me to the Lord was "A Glimmer of Hope." Though he's my uncle, I can say he is a man of integrity. I know he is a man just like any other man– saved by grace–but, he is not carnal minded.

My transition from Detroit to California has been very difficult. I was exposed to the carnal, fleshly side of some preachers like never before. Pastor Anderson was protective of his flock. He didn't allow just anyone to come and preach at Greater Rose of Sharon. He had to know them.

He preached and taught many of us until we grew up and matured in the Lord. So when it came time for me to leave the nest, I had a sure foundation to build upon. I thank God for the teaching of Pastor Anderson and his wife. I also appreciate every bishop, elder and mother of Great Lakes Jurisdiction of Michigan who ever spoke a word of truth into my life. I especially appreciate the teaching of my grandparents because when things get shaky, I know I can stand on God's Word.

> *Heaven and earth shall pass away but my words shall not pass away.* (Matthew 24:35)

SOMETHING IS GOING TO HAPPEN

April 7th was my first visit to Greater Bethany. I was in search of new direction. I was not confused by what happened at the church, but I knew that I needed some instruction. I had learned how to adapt to change.

God moved swiftly this time in moving me out. You can not fast and pray and lay before God on a continuous basis and He not move. Something is going to happen. When you're seeking God for the manifestation of His power, you have to know that He is going to show up. Furthermore, I expect God to move. I never know what He is going to do, but I expect Him to do something. This may sound strange to some people, but when you are a soldier you just take orders. When the command comes to move out, you just do it.

God knew that I needed covering and instruction, so He led me to Greater Bethany. He also knew that my strength was being depleted. And, it was not being restored where I was attending. His little transplant had taken root in California. But, the ground was becoming dry and parched.

Pastor Anderson always said, "Whenever you give out of strength, you know where to come to get it replenished." But, I knew I should not have to go back to Detroit just to get spiritual food. God has some men and women of integrity out here in California.

Preaching is not entertainment.

> *It is the spirit that quickeneth; the flesh profiteth nothing: the words that I speak unto you, they are spirit and they are life.*
> (John 6:63)

> *For the word of God is quick and powerful, and sharper than any two-edged sword, piercing even to the dividing asunder of soul and spirit, and of the joints and marrow and is a discerner of the thoughts and intents of the heart.* (Hebrews 4:12)

WHEN FAITH BECOMES GLORY

I needed a word from the Lord. That Sunday, Bishop Jones preached "The Power of Knowing When Faith Becomes Glory." It encouraged and strengthened me in my spirit. The Word lifted me. It was so refreshing. It was like a soaking rain. And, I took it all in. God knew He needed to fortify me. So, while Bishop was praying he said, "God, someone came to be strengthened. Now Lord, give us an unbreakable spirit." The Word and prayer were so powerful. They were enough for me to say, "OK. God, You have led me to water to drink. And, I thank You. Give me strength to drive to Los Angeles for the morning and evening services." He gave it to me.

Sunday, April 14th, Bishop preached, "The Spirit of Glory is Resting Upon You." The Lord had led me to a church where I could receive water. He had led me to a church where I could be fed.

I needed clarity of this new development in my life. And, I needed strength to get through this ongoing situation with my youngest son. I needed a teacher who could give me instructions.

Most of the people I had met in California are not where I am spiritually. And, please do not misunderstand me. That statement is not a put down. I am not lifting myself up. But, some people are still trying to climb up the ladder of position in the church. Most are still spiritual babes.

I'm so glad God knows where we all are in Him. He does care. He knows when to send the right word, at the right time, for you. During Bishop's closing remarks he said, "God is being glorified in you. You're not a spiritual dwarf. You're not leaning on folk now. Your strength level is different. You have to be dealt with differently." He preached so profoundly. It was God speaking, through him, to me. It was awesome.

Bishop Jones prayed, "Now Lord, I pray that the direction will come from You; that the voice they hear will be Yours. Whatever they respond to, let it be You. Drown out every other voice, except Your voice. Sitting at the place of decision, take out every other sound. And, let Your voice be the only voice heard in their mind."

I was so moved. It's like the spirit of God overshadowed me. God is so great. He is greatly to be praised. On the drive home, I could only think about the message and that prayer. The prayer was so anointed. I know God is directing my life. I know He is in control. I know He is ordering my steps.

I wrote a letter of resignation to the pastors of Chapel of Praise. I tried to explain why I had to leave. I stated that you couldn't take someone who has graduated from middle and high school, then put them back into elementary school. Life is not like that. College may be difficult and appear to be intimidating, but there are new challenges that must be faced. God does not take us backwards, but constantly pulls us forward and upward.

God gave me the understanding that there were new lessons for me to learn. I had to continue to mature in Him and in His power. I informed them that my leaving was painful for me. Growth is painful. But I am determined to fulfill whatever purpose God has for me.

> *Howbeit that was not first which is spiritual, but that which is natural; and afterward that which is spiritual.*
>
> (I Corinthians 15:46)

A WORD IN DUE SEASON

I asked God, "Why the struggle? Why another move?" He brought to my mind this passage of Scripture:

And Isaac departed thence, and pitched his tent in the valley of Ge-rar and dwelt there. And Isaac digged again the wells of water, which they had digged in the days of Abraham his father; for the Philistines had stopped them after the death of Abraham: and he called their names after the names by which his father had called them. And Isaac's servants digged in the valley, and found there a well of springing water. And the herdmen of Ge-rar did strive with Isaac's herdmen, saying, the water is ours: and he called the name of the well E-sek; because they strove with him. And they digged another well, and strove for that also: and he called the name of it Sit-nah. And he removed from thence, and digged another well; and for that they strove not: and he called the name of it Re-ho-both; and he said, for now the Lord hath made room for us, and we shall be fruitful in the land. (Genesis 26:17-22)

I truly thank God for His Word and His direction. He has led me to that place. God said in His Word, *a man's gift maketh room for him, and bringeth him before great men.* (Proverbs 18:16) My grandmother held onto that Scripture and so do I. Where He leads me I will follow.

April 21st I attended Greater Bethany for the third time. Bishop got up as they were raising the offering. He said he needed to pray for some people. He called up the New Members Committee and gave them instructions, "Now there are some people that are coming from other persuasions that are already saved and filled with the Holy Ghost. You don't have to re-indoctrinate them. They have already been indoctrinated from wherever they are coming from. You just need to take them in. Those that are un-churched, you can take through the process of indoctrination." The Lord put in my spirit right then that I could join this church. I knew He had given me a church home.

I was brought up in the Church of God in Christ. For me to leave the church of my birth to join another denomination is more than a notion. But, I am following the leading of the Holy Ghost. Holiness is not a denomination; it is a way of life. Bishop Jones is preaching holiness. He is declaring the truth of God's Word. Christ has only one body–the church, His bride. We the people are the church. I believe God is bringing His church together.

A DIVINE APPOINTMENT

On Sunday, May 19th, I attended the New Members Class at eight o'clock. Then, I went across the street to the main sanctuary for morning worship. I sat next to a woman who was not a member of the church. However, after Bishop prayed, she started a conversation with me. I advised her that I was a new member, so I didn't know where the new church was going to be located.

The visitor mentioned that she was from Oklahoma and was here visiting her sister. She mentioned her sister was at West Angeles, but she just wanted to come to hear Bishop Jones. Hearing she was from Oklahoma, I told her that I have a son in jail, in Sapulpa. When I learned that she was from Sapulpa. I almost hollered, "There are black people in Sapulpa?!" She laughed and told me that there are about five hundred or so. I laughed, "Do you believe this! God is a wonder. He is awesome."

We got into the service. Bishop preached, "My Life is Coming Together!" I shouted and praised the God of my salvation. During the offering, she suggested that we exchange addresses and telephone numbers. She inquired as to when I was planning to visit my son? I told her in the next three or four weeks. She told me call her. She would pick me up from the airport and take me to the jail. She has a large four-bedroom house, and welcomed me to stay with her. She asked me my son's name so that she could call and check on him. She belongs to a Church of God in Christ there. Then, she had to leave to meet her sister.

I am so in awe of God. I just kept thinking, "Now it's time for me to go see my son. God, I thank You! You are truly a wonder in my soul. You are my provider. You are my way maker. You are God and there is none like You!"

When Bishop finished his message, he instructed us to hold someone by both hands and pray for that individual. The woman on my right side reached for my hands and we began to pray. After the prayer, she pulled me to herself and embraced me. She began to tell me that God said for me to write. That God had given me something to write that would be a blessing to a lot of people. She told me to start writing now! She said it with such conviction that something jumped in my spirit. I replied, "I receive that word." A friend and his mother both previously told me I needed to write. Now, God had sent a stranger to confirm what He had already told me to do.

I started writing everyday after that. It's like the Holy Ghost was pushing me from way down on the inside. He would wake me up at one or two o'clock in the morning to write. My thoughts were flowing. He put that sense of urgency back in my spirit.

On Sunday, May 26th, the Spirit led me to be baptized again. So, I was baptized at Greater Bethany Community Church in Jesus' name, according to Acts 2:38. It was a wonderfully, different experience for me. It was different because of the level of spiritual growth and understanding that God has given me.

It amazes me that God not only transplanted me from Detroit to California to work in another part of His vineyard. Now, He has grafted me into another part of the body of Christ.

> *For though I be free from all men, yet have I made myself servant unto all, that I might gain the more.* (I Corinthians 9:19)

6 When Faith Becomes Glory

I needed to see my son. He needed to see someone from his family, so he wouldn't lose hope. I prayed to God for strength and courage to go. It meant going to another place I had never been before–and going alone. I finally got up my nerve to go visit in July. I prayed for God to give me favor with men.

I called the Sapulpa County sheriff to advise him I would be coming from California. I asked if he would make an exception and allow me to visit my son longer than the normal fifteen minutes on Sunday. He agreed and asked me to call him whenever I got there.

I called the woman whom I had met at church that lives in Sapulpa. She remembered me, but she was on her way to Texas. I asked where the closest hotel to the Sapulpa County Jail was. She told me there was a Motel 6 about fifteen miles from the Tulsa Airport. And, the jail was about another fifteen miles from the Motel 6.

I arrived in Tulsa, Oklahoma about 11:30, at night. I rented a car. Driving down the highway, I was praying, "God, please let the directions be accurate. Lord, please be with me!" I was crying and praying. It was scary being out on the highway at night alone, especially since I wasn't sure where I was going. But I made it! Thank You, Lord!

The next morning, I asked the motel clerk for directions to the Sapulpa County Jail. I found my way to the jail, but they had taken my son to court in Bristol. I had to drive another thirty miles to the Bristol Courthouse. Thank You, Lord. I made it! I just wanted to sit down anywhere. I was so frazzled. But my son signaled for me to come closer to him.

I was able to sit two rows from my son and look into his eyes. He was smiling. And I could see the hope in his eyes. I was smiling but fighting back tears. Again, I am crying as I'm typing this. I sat through the hearing, but nothing significant happened. I whispered to him that I had to go. I needed to get back up the highway before it got late. It was hard leaving him sitting there. But I had to go.

I met with his attorney while at the courthouse. He told me that the district attorney had offered my son twenty-five years. When he said that, I almost broke down. I told him, "I can't handle that." He said my son told him he wasn't accepting that.

My son didn't know I had made arrangements to see him on an off visitation day. I needed God to give me strength. I needed to recover quickly from speaking with his attorney. I still had to get through Saturday and Sunday. The Spirit put a song in my heart, and I was singing down the highway.

ANOTHER DELAY

I made it back to Sapulpa and went to the county jail. I informed the deputy who I was and who I came to visit. I explained that I got in from California the night before. And, explained that I had made arrangements with the Sheriff to visit with my son for a half an hour that day, Friday. You know the devil was mad.

Don't let anyone fool you, prejudice is alive and well. Now, I had to deal with this prejudice issue, up close and in person. I was in a position of having to take some mess I wouldn't normally take. I had to endure this man talking to me in a manner that I wouldn't normally allow. Talk about a humbling experience? God allows you to be put in positions where you can't do anything but pray and ask

Him to keep you. God will allow you to get in situations where you can't do anything but trust Him.

The deputy did not believe me. He said, I haven't been told anything. So, take a seat until I can get the sheriff on the telephone." I was sitting there and the tears started streaming down. I needed to leave. I was becoming overwhelmed with the situation. I'm so glad God is the strength of my life. He always gives me a word when I need Him. When I feel I can't make it, He fortifies me. I remembered His Word. I have learned how to stand in the strength of His Word.

> *And he said unto me, my grace is sufficient for thee: for my strength is made perfect in weakness.* (II Corinthians 12:9a)

I asked about a restaurant, so I could get something to eat, and then come back. Someone told me that I should hurry because it closed at 2:00. As I was leaving, I saw the bus pulling up with the prisoners, but I kept going. I needed to get away. I needed to compose myself.

When I returned to the jail, the deputy had decided he would allow me to see my son for thirty minutes. He gave me strict instructions that there was to be no touching, whatsoever, or the visit would be ended. They brought my son in. He was so surprised! He sat right next to me. I had to sit on my hands. We were so close, yet I couldn't touch him. I couldn't hug him or kiss him. That was painful! He was concerned about me, and wanted to know if I was OK.

We talked. He explained some things to me. He was smiling the entire time. I was so glad to see him. I told him I had been singing all the way down the highway when I left him in court. Then, I just started singing to him. I sung, "I won't complain." I was singing softly in that little room, sitting next to my son.

Have you ever witnessed God break the spirit in a person? I have. While sitting there, singing to my son, the atmosphere changed. People were coming in the room to talk with the deputy that had earlier talked so rough to me. Now he was telling them to be quiet and come back later. He let me visit for about forty-five minutes. God is a wonder! Only God can move on the heart of a man to give you favor.

The king's heart is in the hand of the Lord, as the rivers of water: he turneth it whithersoever he will. (Proverbs 21:1)

Months had passed. Time was moving on and nothing was happening. The case was being postponed from week to week, then every two weeks. I asked my son if the attorney was fighting for him or what? He didn't know what the attorney was doing. But, he finally came to the conclusion that the attorney didn't know what he was doing.

Nevertheless, the attorney wanted another $2,500.00 because the case was going to trial. I had already paid him over $4,000.00. I told him, I wasn't giving him another dime. He hadn't done anything to really represent my son.

We didn't know how to get a recommendation for another attorney in Oklahoma. My son was using an attorney he had seen in court. This situation was hard. We didn't know who to trust. I was sending money to a stranger and I really didn't like that. There was no way for me to find out anything about him. I needed to have some checks and balances going on, but I didn't. I told my son I have been seeking the Lord for direction. I'm praying for mercy everyday. And, I need God to give us some direction.

The holiday season was here. My family and I made it through Thanksgiving Day just grateful to God that my son was still alive. We were all holding on. Although 2002 was rough, God has been good! He has been faithful! I was going to church and praising Him in spite of what was happening. He had provided for me. He had protected me. He had blessed me with health and strength. I went to work every day, except for my vacations. The storms were raging, but my soul was anchored in God. He kept me strong by His Word.

FIGHTING ON

Bishop Jones was preaching under the anointing of the Holy Ghost. I took in every word because it is the only way I could make it. Sometimes, my son called me on Sunday's. I would tell him just about everything Bishop said, especially, when it was an encouraging message to lift our spirits. Or, sometimes, the message was telling us to fight to hold onto our minds or our faith.

I had been fighting hard. I was fighting to keep my peace of mind, fighting to maintain my health. I was pushing and pressing my way through this. I couldn't break. I thank God for knowing we have a merciful and faithful high priest in Jesus.

Once again, God had given me unwavering faith in Him. He gave me strength to stand and fight for the souls of my children. The devil brought to my mind that the Lord loved Jacob and hated Esau. I had to bind him and cast him out of my mind. I was crying out to God and asking Him to keep us covered under the blood of Christ. I was reading His Word every day. It was my only defense. I would speak God's Word back to Him.

> *Thou wilt keep him in perfect peace, whose mind is stayed on thee: because he trusteth in thee.* (Isaiah 26:3)

> *Behold the eye of the Lord is upon them that fear him, upon them that hope in his mercy. Let thy mercy, O Lord, be upon us, according as we hope in thee.* (Psalms 33:18, 22)

I would tell God, "My son is trusting in You. My trust is in You. Our hope is in You." I had been in a spiritual battle all year long, but I was still standing. I still had joy and peace in the Holy Ghost.

December 1, 2002, Bishop Jones preached "It's the Right Time."

> *But when the fullness of the time was come, God sent forth his Son, made of a woman, made under the law, To redeem them that were under the law, that we might receive the adoption of sons.* (Galatians 4:4-5)

A SHIFT IN MY SPIRIT

This message was sent straight from Heaven. I say that because there was a shift by the Holy Ghost in my spirit. That is the only way to explain what happened. I had been praying all year for mercy. That was all I could ask God for. My son was guilty of wrong doing, so all I could ask was that God be merciful to him. I prayed that God would not allow the devil to destroy his life. He was not a bad person. Like many people, he had made some bad choices; and, he was paying the price for it.

Bishop explained, "The devil moves in the darkness. But in the fullness of time, God sent His Son, Jesus. When God gets ready to break the power of the devil in your life, He uses the power of the miracle. When your situation is getting worse, worse means its closer to the miracle." The message was powerful. He preached so hard.

He stayed on top of the mountain for a while. When he finally started coming down, the Spirit in him was ministering to the hearts of God's people. He reminded us that satan has no respect for any of us. He comes to steal, to kill and to destroy.

As always, at the end of the message, he prayed. "Lord, we're before You at the right time, because we've come from difficulty to impossibility. That means the next step is miracle. We believe You for a miracle. You have sustained us when it was difficulty. And, You have kept us when it was impossibility. Now, we need a miracle, in the name of Jesus. My brother needs a miracle. My sister needs a miracle. We all need a miracle. I need a miracle. I speak it from my soul! I speak it from my spirit!"

God anointed Bishop so. The Spirit of the Lord moved in him. Whatever you needed, you could have gotten it that day. I certainly did. I was overwhelmed. I stand in awe of God all the time. I worship and I praise Him. I love Him. I adore Him. There is no other God. He is God alone.

My prayers changed. Now, I was asking God for a miracle, not just mercy. I wanted and needed a miracle. I was still walking around the building where I work on my breaks. I would pray and I would sing. I would sing, "I'm Looking for a Miracle." I would tell God, "I expect the impossible because you are the God of miracles. There is nothing too hard for You. And I believe You're still in the miracle-working business." I would drive home singing, "I have faith to see the invisible, expect the impossible, receive the incredible–faith that can conquer anything." I'm telling you the Holy Ghost made a shift in my spirit.

December 16th was my son's birthday and he spent it in jail. It had been a rough day for me, thinking about him and his life. I had never expected this. I was praying, "Lord, please do not let my son die in that horrible place." My oldest son, who is still in the Marine Corp, called to check on me and find out if I had heard anything from his brother. No matter what is going on with him and the Corp, he always makes the time to call or email me to check on his brother.

GOD IS THE GOD OF MIRACLES

My son went to court again on December 18th. His attorney told him that he knew the district attorney and they could possibly work out a deal. The deal was a $10,000.00 fine with five years probation–and we only had to pay a percentage of that, $2,500.00. That was a miracle! The deal had changed from the possibility of twenty-five years in prison to possibly five years probation. I tell you God is the God of miracles. God was moving!

My son told me that he understood that I had given out so much financially, and if I couldn't come up with the money that he would be OK. He would be satisfied, as long as they would give him a decent out date. He needed to know this trial was going to be over. He resolved within himself to take whatever punishment he had to take, as long as he felt it was fair. I understood him, but I told him to hold on. God is moving now, so don't give up on Him. Keep the faith. He said he hadn't given up. He even tried to reassure me that he would be all right.

I was walking at work when the Lord put in my spirit to stand still. He reminded me that He didn't bring the children of Israel to the Red Sea to have them drown or to be overtaken by Pharaoh and his army. He was telling me that He had not brought us this far to leave us now. "So, stand still and see the salvation of the Lord."

A friend had asked me if I would come and teach a Bible study in her home. So I do. God has blessed our endeavors. I see spiritual growth in the women I teach. I don't talk about my son's situation with them often, even though they know about it. Talking about something I can't change doesn't help me. It causes more stress. But, that particular night, as I was closing in prayer, I asked them to remember my son. I shared with them Bishop's message and told them God had given us a miracle.

I told them I'm trusting God to help me come up with another $2,500.00 because I had just paid out $2,500.00 to get this new attorney. My son had taken my advice and wrote to a few family members in Detroit. They sent me some money to help get him this new attorney. So, there was no one else to turn to.

Finally, I gave up the last of the money I had been holding for my book project. But, he is worth the sacrifice. I wasn't worried about it. I needed my son to have hope. And I believed God was going to provide whatever we needed. He knows I trust Him to do it, so I don't worry about money.

MIRACLE NUMBER TWO

On Christmas Eve, a friend called and left a message for me saying, God told her to give me the $2,500.00 that I needed. I was in shock. I was in tears. I was so stunned that I played the message over and over, but I wouldn't call her back. Bishop has said you can't do anything with a promise but wait for it. I thanked God for the phone call and went to bed.

Christmas morning, my friend called and told me to come over to pick up the check. Since I was going to another friend's house for dinner, I said I would stop by on my way. When I walked into her house, she just handed me a Christmas card with the check inside. We hugged each other and cried. She said to me, "You know it had to be God because I have never given anyone this amount of money before." When I told my husband that God told me to give it to you, he just said, "Do what you have to do." Again she said, "So, you know that was God." This is miracle number two. And, I'm looking for the third one in the name of the Father, of the Son and of the Holy Ghost!

God has done so much for me I cannot tell it all. This was supposed to be one of my short clusters of faith stories. But God is so great! He is too great to be contained in any book. This book is a testimony of His faithfulness in our lifetime, not just biblical times. God is faithful that promised. God still works miracles. God not only grants us His favor, but He gives us favor with men! Deliverance is just around the corner. The prison door will come open! I'm expecting it any day now.

"MAMA, THEY LET ME OUT!"

March 10, 2003, my son called me about 11:30 p.m. "Mama, they let me out!" I was stunned. He said, "They called about twenty of us out of our cells, took us before a judge, and let us out on a Personal Recognizance Bond." You know I started crying.

I wanted to know where he was and all the details. He was at a Days Inn. A young man, who had been in jail with him, helped him to get a room and something to eat. My son told him he would pay him back the next day. My son's wife flew from Detroit to Oklahoma with their daughter, whom my son had never held.

On Wednesday, March 12th my son flew home to Detroit. He is walking free among those that love him. Free! This is miracle number three! God, I thank You! I thank You! I thank You! I praise You. I magnify You. I lift You up. I lift You higher than people, places or circumstances in my life because You are God. I love You and I adore You.

Jesus questioned Peter's love for Him.

> *So when they had dined, Jesus saith to Simon Peter, Simon son of Jonas, lovest thou me more than these? He saith unto him, yea, Lord; thou knowest that I love thee. He saith unto him, feed my lambs. He saith to him again the second time, Simon son of Jonas, lovest thou me? He saith unto him, yea Lord; thou knowest that I love thee. He saith unto him, feed my sheep.*
>
> (John 21:15-16)

I know I'm in the place the Lord wants me to be because Bishop Jones is a man of integrity and a shepherd that loves God's sheep. When he preaches the Word of God, I get fed. New growth is beginning to show as is evidenced by this book.

Thank You, Holy Ghost, for the push down in my spirit. Again, thank you Bishop for declaring the Word of God. I pray that God blesses you, richly. And, I thank all of you for the privilege of sharing some of my experiences with you. I hope and pray you all were blessed.

About the Author

Evangelist Cheryl L. Black was born and raised in Detroit, Michigan. She grew up in a Christian home with her grandparents. She is the mother of five children and has ten grandchildren.

Evangelist Black, under the leadership of Pastor C. T. Anderson, was an active member of Greater Rose of Sharon C.O.G.I.C. until her move to California, a few years ago.

She accepted the call from the Lord to teach and taught Sunday school for over seventeen years. She received her Evangelist license in 1988. She was a district and jurisdictional worker in Great Lakes Ecclesiastical Jurisdiction of Michigan, under the late Bishop C. L. Anderson, Jr. and Mother Merle R. Cranford. Evangelist Black is currently a member of City of Refuge, formerly known as Greater Bethany Community Church, where Bishop Noel Jones is the pastor.

Evangelist Black carries a burden for the souls of our sons and our daughters. She believes that just because our children become adults does not mean they should be left to their own imaginations.

They need someone to listen and to counsel them, or they will be destroyed.

Evangelist Black believes parents should never stop talking to their children, because the devil never stops. If you open up and share your life with them, it may help them not to make some of the same mistakes you made. It may cause them to think along the way. Even if they fall into the traps of the enemy, they should be encouraged in the faith. Give them hope. Remember, charity begins at home, and then spreads abroad.

For bulk purchasing or speaking appointments you may contact Evangelist Cheryl Black via email at clblack8985@netzero.net.